ObamaCare Simplified for Your Business

Chuck Kimball

Payday
24/7 Institute Press

ObamaCare Simplified for Your Business

Published by 24/7 Institute Press
Pensacola, FL

Library of Congress Cataloging in Publication Data

ISBN 978-0615807560

For quantity purchases of this book contact:

Payday 24/7 Institute
4490 North W Street
Pensacola, FL 32505
(850) 912-8884
www.247institute.com
www.paydayhr.com

Book and cover design by Matt Arnold, Payday

Printed in the United States of America

10 9 8 7 6 5 4 3 2 1

Table of Contents

Foreword

The ObamaCare legislation is without question the single greatest (and most confusing) legislation I've witnessed in my 23 years in business. Not only is the law long, convoluted, and confusing, it is even difficult for well-trained professionals to know where to start.

That was until now.

Chuck Kimball has demystified ObamaCare for my employees and me. This well-thought-out, high-content book gives me the starting point I need to better understand the upsides and the potential downsides of healthcare coverage.

No one book can answer all my questions on how to handle ObamaCare. Chuck's book gets me on the right track with the boost in confidence I need to make the right decisions and take the right steps for my people, their families and me.

My prayer is that this book will do the same for you.

Mike Hill
Independent Business Owner
Graduate – US Air Force Academy

Introduction

In my 15 years in the HR industry, without a doubt, the Patient Protection and Affordable Care Act (PPACA), known as ObamaCare, is the largest piece of game-changing legislation ever passed down for employers to deal with. Certainly, the 2700-plus-page bill impacts every employer in one facet or another. In *ObamaCare Simplified*, my goal is to take this massive legislation and break it down into manageable chunks that will help you overcome the challenges, as well as take advantage of some of the benefits.

It is my hope that you'll find this a simple, objective look at the legislation and it will help you apply ObamaCare in your business.

When I ask business owners why they chose to start or run the business they own, I get a variety of answers. For some, the business evolved from a hobby they had a passion for, or a skill they developed; and for others, it was a family business that they inherited. I have never heard a business owner tell me that they got into business to handle paperwork and administration!

That's why WE exist! We at Payday excel at handling these back-office functions and allow business owners to focus on their core businesses. With ObamaCare challenges quickly facing employers, it can be overwhelming to the point that they don't have an appropriate amount of time to focus on actually running their business.

We highly recommend that you take those tasks that are unprofitable, time-consuming and generally a strain on your business, and outsource them to an expert or, in our case, a team of experts. Keeping up with the ever-changing healthcare regulations is enough to keep you busy full time, and if you don't give it proper attention, it could cause you to close your business entirely.

At the conclusion of this book are some questions that every business owner needs to be able to answer about their own business in order to stay ahead of the curve. If you aren't prepared now, don't hesitate: You may attend my free 45-minute webinar (ObamaCareWebinar.com), or give us a call and we can help you navigate the confusing world of ObamaCare.

Chuck Kimball, PHR
Payday
866-928-7450
obamacare@paydayhr.com

1
Small or Large Business and Full-Time Employees

In the past, businesses have chosen to define themselves as small or big, medium or giant. Whatever the terminology—it didn't matter—the choice was up to them. ObamaCare takes the liberty of defining what is a small business and what is a large business.

There are surely some businesses out there currently defined as one or the other that wouldn't classify themselves as such, but choice is no longer an option. As defined by ObamaCare, a "small business" is one that has fewer than 50 full-time employees (FTES). These terms are still somewhat deceiving because an employer may have only 10 FTES and hundreds of part-time employees, yet still be considered a small business.

The legislation has a much larger financial impact on those businesses that are considered "large businesses," which is basically any organization with greater than 50 FTES. In the news recently have been stories of businesses reducing staff to drop below this threshold of FTES in order to not have to comply with the legislation. This is one viable strategy for some employers that hover around this magic number of employees.

What is a full-time employee?

Let's answer a question that has not really been addressed on a Federal level until this bill and that is, "What is a full-time employee?" In the past, some states have defined this themselves, but now we have a Federal ruling on the answer to this question.

An employee that is scheduled to work 30 or more hours weekly is how we define a full-time employee. That is a simplified answer. The government has been kind enough to release an 18-page document that goes into great detail as to how to define this question, but most employers can quickly use the 30-hour rule to answer the question. If you have a unique situation or something that falls into a gray area, we would advise you to seek counsel on how to classify your employees.

Hire more employees?

It may not be as common, but many employers are choosing to actually hire more employees as a result of ObamaCare. The reason for the hiring isn't necessarily because of growth, but rather due to the fact that they will be scaling back their FTES, so they will hire more part-time employees. The goal here may not be to drop below the threshold where the law will apply to them, but only to eliminate the cost of providing benefits for as many employees, or the tax penalty, whichever route they decide.

Which is the best path to choose? The answer to that is one that we cannot simplify in this book. This is a complex decision that each business owner must make himself or herself. We encourage you to seek counsel from an experienced HR Professional, Insurance Agent, CPA, Attorney or some combination of these.

2
Grandfathered vs. Non-Grandfathered Plan

When developing an ObamaCare survival roadmap for a client, one of the first things that I attempt to find out is if they currently have a non-grandfathered plan, or if their plan is qualified under the grandfathered provision.

There are a few reasons that this is an important question. The first thing to look at in order to determine if your plan has been grandfathered is how long your plan has been in place with the insurance carrier. You need to ensure that your plan was in place before March 23, 2010, which was the day that ObamaCare was signed into law. Next, check to see if you have changed plans or plan structures (deductible, co-insurance, etc.) after that date. You may think your plan has changed because the carrier has done something like waiving co-pays on preventative care, but surprisingly, that may not have impacted your grandfathered/non-grandfathered status.

Advantages

Providing that you have a grandfathered plan, you must now examine if it is worth revising your options or if you want to keep your current plan. Some advantages of keeping your grandfathered plan could be a "carve-out," which will no longer be available to you after full implementation of ObamaCare. Another advantage of keeping a grandfathered plan would be that you could potentially retain a plan structure, such as a higher or lower deductible, which would not be available to someone currently getting a group plan.

Disadvantages

A potential downside of keeping a grandfathered plan could be employee confusion. Most people have a very limited knowledge of health insurance and how it works; this could become an issue when they hear from someone else that a plan has to meet certain requirements that your grandfathered plan does not have to meet. The only real problem with this is that someone within your organization may have to spend valuable time explaining how your plan is still compliant. The most important reason you may not want to retain grandfathered status is the cost, which will most likely escalate at a faster pace.

Deciding on making a change if you have a grandfathered plan is not something that should be taken lightly or done without good planning. We currently have some clients with both types of plans. Those that retain their grandfathered status have motivating factors that outweigh any potential upside of moving to a non-grandfathered plan. Then, other clients have been happy to modify their plan structure and lose the grandfathered status that they had. Your Health Insurance Agent should be able to review your plan and let you know its current status. Our team of experts is always willing to review your plan and assist you in any way possible.

3
Good Things Come to Those Who Wait ... Just No More than 90 Days

One of the biggest problems that employers face today is employee retention. Many employers, small or large, have addressed the issue of retention, in relation to health insurance, by having an extended waiting period for joining a health insurance plan. In many places an employee must complete 6, 9 or even 12 months of service before they are eligible to participate in a group health plan.

Some industries, no matter how good the culture is, will always be plagued with employee retention issues. For those industries, an extended waiting period has helped them manage costs as well as the administrative burden of constantly adding or removing participants from their group health plan.

No waiting

Under ObamaCare no waiting period may exist that is greater than 90 days. This will be a drastic change for those employers that were opting for employees to wait an entire 12 months before participating.

Using a call center as an example, it is not uncommon for a new employee to make it beyond a 90-day probationary period, yet not exceed 6 months of employment with the company. With this example, under ObamaCare after 2014, this call center would have to allow participation on the group plan, enroll the participant, contribute towards premium, then terminate coverage or offer COBRA all within the 6-month window. The advantage of this is that many employees who may not have stayed 12 months may obtain coverage quickly and be able to seek the medical care they may need.

Additionally, certain large employers will be required to automatically enroll employees in health insurance after the waiting period. This helps eliminate the chance of an employee's enrollment being overlooked.

There is no creative way around this challenge in ObamaCare. If your company currently has a waiting period greater than 90 days, you must begin to plan what this impact is going to have on your business. You may be able to take the path discussed in Chapter 1, making some employees part-time, therefore, not eligible for health insurance.

4
Change Is Coming ... to Your Major Medical Plan

One of the campaign buzzwords that President Obama used during his first campaign was "Change." Like it or not, the result of ObamaCare is going to change your group health insurance plan. Some changes have already taken place and some are still yet to change over an extended timetable all the way through 2018, with the largest changes happening in 2014. Below are some of the biggest changes that have either already happened or will be happening soon.

- Dependent care up to age 26 (2010)
- No charge for preventative care (2010)
- Annual Deductible Maximum now $2,000/year individual or $4,000/year family (2014)
- Annual Out of Pocket Maximum now $5,000/year individual or $10,000/year family (2014)
- Rate changes no longer allowed based upon gender or health condition (2014)

- FSA contributions by employer capped at $2,500/year (2014)
- Waiting period maximum of 90 days (discussed in Chapter 3) (2014)
- Limited Benefit Plans (Mini-Medical) no longer compliant (2014)

Some of these changes have already had tremendous impact on group health insurance. Carriers are currently working to design plans that will be fully compliant with ObamaCare in 2014. As the IRS, Department of Health and Human Services and Congress continue to add details to the bill, there is no doubt things will continue to change. This is the main reason that carriers are not overly anxious to release their new plan structures, since they do not know if they will be forced to change them again.

It is vitally important that you stay on top of these changes as they continue to be released. Our team of Certified ObamaCare Advisors constantly educates themselves to keep clients apprised of these changes. You may be part of an association or group that also keeps up on these items, however, it is important to make sure that you consider these changes as they apply specifically to your business.

5
Comply or Be Taxed

ObamaCare was found to be a constitutional law under the taxing power of Congress. The tax impact to businesses of this legislation is substantial. It can be both positive and negative, depending on the size of your business. Those businesses that are classified as small to medium businesses (less than 50 FTES) can receive a direct tax write-off for part of the premium that they contribute towards major medical health insurance. Larger businesses do not have the same positive reinforcement. Instead, they face a tax penalty if they are not offering qualified health insurance or if their plans are not "affordable."

Small-/medium-sized businesses

Businesses that have less than 25 employees can currently receive an income tax credit for up to 35% of what they pay toward premiums of health insurance. Even Not-For-Profit entities can get an incentive for offering benefits at a lower 25% rate. This credit is set to increase to 50% for a for-profit company and 35% for a Not-For-Profit company in 2014 and beyond. There are some calculations that also come into play with average wages paid to employees, so I would not suggest assuming that this will apply to you. As each situation is different, you should get clarification from a professional who understands these concepts before going forward.

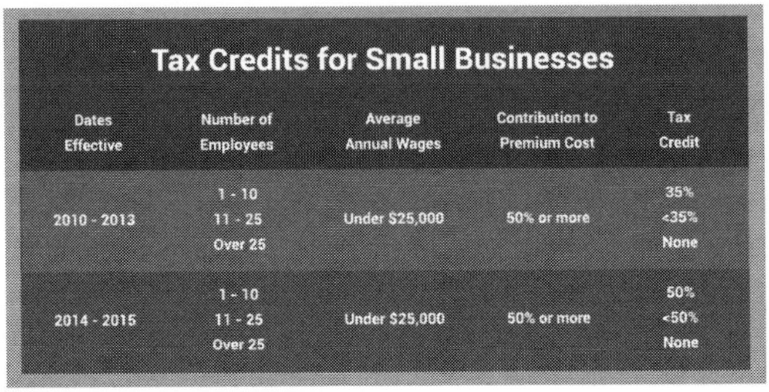

Tax Credits for Small Businesses

Dates Effective	Number of Employees	Average Annual Wages	Contribution to Premium Cost	Tax Credit
2010 - 2013	1 - 10 11 - 25 Over 25	Under $25,000	50% or more	35% <35% None
2014 - 2015	1 - 10 11 - 25 Over 25	Under $25,000	50% or more	50% <50% None

Medium-sized/large businesses

A business that has greater or equal to 50 FTES will now be required to offer plans that are compliant with ObamaCare. As an employer, if your plan is not compliant with the law, or if it is too costly for your employees, as soon as you have one employee that receives the premium assistance tax credit, you will be penalized in the form of a tax. The business will be taxed either $3,000 for each employee receiving a credit or $750 for each of their employees total, whichever is less. Should a business choose to completely waive coverage, the tax penalty is $2,000 for every full-time employee after subtracting the first 30 full-time employees.

Individual

For those smaller businesses with too few employees to offer health coverage, or that may be just a sole proprietor, you or your employees may be subject to a tax, also. Any individual that is deemed able to afford coverage must obtain acceptable health insurance or face an individual tax. The tax on individuals is a stair-step plan. In 2014, the tax penalty for an individual not maintaining coverage will be a modest $95 per adult in the household, or 1% of annual income, whichever is greater. In 2015, that tax rises to $495 or 2% of annual income per adult. The final increase that has been identified in 2016 is $750 or 2.5% of annual income per adult. Children are subject to a penalty of half these figures, up to a family maximum of $2,250. After 2016, the tax is set to increase in line with the annual cost of living adjustment.

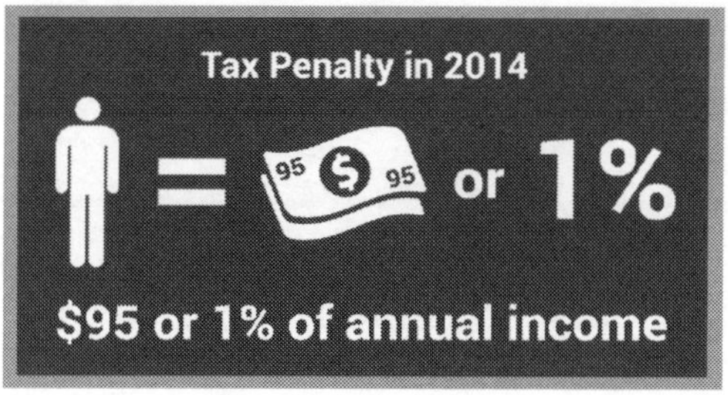

Can you avoid the tax? There are a few qualifying options to avoid having to pay the tax, whether it be as a business or an individual. With this ever-evolving bill, I suggest that, even if you can qualify under one of the loopholes today, it will probably not last. It is likely that, as loopholes are discovered and taken advantage of, those options will cease to exist.

As a business owner, the best thing that you can do is to be prepared. Analyze your plan options today as to how many employees will subject you to the tax penalty. Work with someone that is experienced in coming up with creative solutions to help your company take dollars away from a tax penalty and put them towards the bottom line.

6
The Devil's in the Details: New Forms to Complete and Old Ones to Adapt

If you are familiar with the Department of Homeland Security form I-9 (Employment Eligibility), maybe this will help you to understand how things work. The form was modified as part of the government's "Paperwork Reduction Act" and, if you can guess what that did, you receive an "A" in bureaucracy. The act ended up causing an additional page to be added to this form that must be completed by every new employee that is hired to work in the United States. If you didn't think that a 2700-plus-page bill such as the PPACA would add additional paperwork to be completed, you are sorely mistaken.

W-2 forms

As a business owner, you understand that every year on or before January 31st, you must have all W-2 forms completed and postmarked to all current and former employees; that is nothing new. The change is in how health insurance premiums are to be shown on all W-2 forms. This change was first voluntary on 2012 W-2 forms and then became mandatory on 2013 forms for any employer that employed more than 250 employees during the previous year.

In 2014 and beyond, it will apply to all employers. Any business that contributes dollars toward employee health insurance or other specified benefits are now required to show those contributions on the W-2 form. The addition of these dollars does not increase the tax that the employee pays; however, it is designed to show the employee the benefit of the health insurance that is provided by their employer. The concept is not all bad, however, this is an additional, potentially time-consuming, effort required by the employer.

As with other areas of non-compliance, if an employer does not comply, there are penalties that go along with those shortfalls. Certainly, if you are using some type of software to produce your W-2 forms, it should know where to place those contributions and how to account for them; however, if you are unsure of what to put into the software, you may still be at risk of non-compliance.

Summary of benefits

Beginning with your 2013-year renewal of your health insurance plan, employers are required to complete and provide a Summary of Benefits form to distribute to employees. This form is a 6- to 8-page document with plan specifics about each health insurance plan that is offered. These forms are not required to be completed by your health insurance carrier, but rather by you as the employer. As with W-2 forms, if you do not comply with this provision of the PPACA, you will face non-compliance fines and penalties. Most experienced agents are capable of assisting you with preparing these forms; however, since it is not their responsibility to do so, you will probably need to contact them and seek assistance.

There are other areas of paperwork compliance within the bill, but these are the largest two, and one of these will eventually impact all employers if it hasn't impacted you already. It is vital to the sustainability of your business that you prepare for these changes well in advance. I suggest that you work with a seasoned professional who is knowledgeable about both health insurance and the human resource implications of these new regulations.

7
Get Out the Crystal Ball: A Prediction About the Future of Health Insurance

Let me start off by saying that I am not an economist, nor am I an insurance actuary. I am simply a seasoned professional in human resources and insurance. My thoughts and opinions about the impact of ObamaCare are not legal opinions, but rather well-educated opinions.

When ObamaCare first was drafted and signed into law through the backdoor reconciliation process, many started to think about what the goal of the bill was. The idea that each individual should have health insurance is a great idea, however not a right. Some first thought that, since our government knew they likely would not pass a law with a single-payer health system, making care accessible to all was a noble way of accomplishing their goal. I suggest that passing this bill was a successful way to accomplish their goal of a single-payer health care system. If this bill stands as it is, I would imagine that in less than 10 years, all private health insurance companies will cease to exist as we know them today, and here is why.

Pre-existing conditions

With carriers not permitted to decline coverage or certain treatments because of a pre-existing condition, they will be forced to insure anyone no matter the health condition. Obviously, this is going to increase the cost of what health insurers are paying out in claims. Likely in 2014, insurers will see a huge influx of new customers; however, they will primarily be only those who could not get coverage before. For example, an individual who had cancer will now be able to immediately enroll in coverage and begin getting treatments.

Deductible decreases

With deductibles being forced to drop, this will cause more exposure on the insurance company. This will result, of course, in an immediate increase in premiums to those who must now decrease their deductibles. Many individuals have migrated to "high-deductible" plans that are lower in premiums and afford them to only seek medical care when it is really necessary. With these plans going away and insurance carriers paying out more in claims, this will again impact the bottom line.

Rise in premiums

With the rise in premiums from the above two items, I suggest that many "healthy" individuals will begin to waive health insurance and pay any tax penalty that they will be subject to. Even at the highest tax penalty in 2016 of $750 per adult, that is significantly lower than what the premium would equal over the course of a year. Today, for a 30-year-old male, let's say, for the case of argument, that his monthly premium for a PPACA compliant plan is $300. With that amount over 12 months, he would pay $3,600 per year in premiums.

If this individual is healthy, why not just pay the penalty and then, if he was to get sick, he could just go get coverage then. There is no penalty for being irresponsible with this new structure. This effect will ultimately result in health insurers with mainly "un-healthy" individuals on their books. With this result, health insurance companies can only be expected to remain sustainable for only so long.

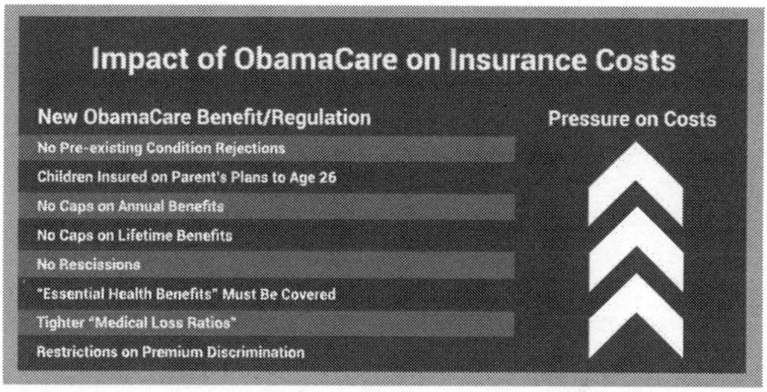

These points suggest that a future administration may be "forced" to either bailout the health insurance industry or implement a universal healthcare option administered by the government. You can expect a tax increase to cover the cost of this new benefit. Although President Obama will not see the ultimate end result during his presidency, he will no doubt see it in his lifetime.

8

The 2013 Impact to Your Business: Paperwork to Prepare

This is the last chance that you have to prepare for the upcoming big changes in 2014. Many business owners from the time that ObamaCare was mentioned, chose to wait, thinking that the bill would not last. Many felt like it would not make it through the Supreme Court, some felt it would not make it through a re-election and some are still fighting it in court today. Like it or not, it is here and you must comply with it now unless we are surprised at a later date. As mentioned in Chapter 6, there are new forms to comply with in 2013 and I suggest that you begin preparing for those changes now.

Prepare and communicate wisely

Review your current group health insurance plan to see if it is going to be PPACA compliant in 2014. This is the opportune time to being preparing for the changes that are going to come. Prepare your employees if things are going to change. Maybe you are going to have to decrease what you contribute towards health insurance, change the waiting periods for insurance, or sadly, maybe you are going to cancel your group coverage totally. Possibly, yours is a company that is going to begin offering coverage now and taking advantage of the tax incentive. Whatever the case, don't hesitate on preparing and communicating with your employees what you are going to do.

Analyze your current workforce to see if streamlining some things may be able to allow you to change some of your employees to a now part-time status, or eliminate a position or two if it will help to keep you below the threshold of being forced to comply with ObamaCare. As with the other options, if this is your plan, it is best to communicate these changes to your employees before the last minute. I recommend using the RACI method as implemented by Joel Manby with Herschend Family Entertainment.

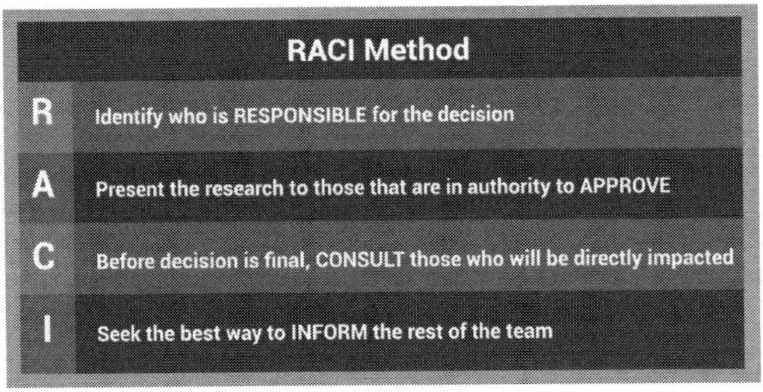

Manby suggests that, by implementing the RACI method when rolling out a decision that will impact many, this is the best method and actually decreases the overall time from decision to buy-in. By including more people in this decision-making process, it will absolutely increase buy-in from everyone else when a difficult decision has to be made. If there is one topic that people take personally, it is their health insurance. The more you can prepare them for changes, the better. 2013 is the time to start preparing your teams for changes, so when 2014 hits, everyone will be ready.

9

The 2014 Impact to Your Business: Persevere and Press On

Hopefully, by the time 2014 comes around, you will have prepared and will be ready. What does 2014 look like to your business? Have you planned and prepared for potential changes in your staffing needs, maybe reducing the number of staff or changing parts of your team to a part-time status? If you haven't taken the time to assess your current situation, the time is now! 2014 will be the most transformative year in the health insurance industry, and a year of change as to how businesses handle employment benefits due to this legislation.

Some good news is that at least everyone, including your competition, has to deal with the same issues that you are now. Maybe you haven't been offering insurance up to now but decided, with the increased tax incentive, now is the time. Some employers will be canceling their group plans in 2014 and just dealing with the consequences, whatever they may be. The decision on whether or not you should cancel your plan, continue to offer coverage, or start a new plan is not something that cannot simply be decided without serious forethought and planning.

Does the fact that you currently offer health insurance make your business more competitive in attracting the best employees? If you no longer have this benefit, will you be more likely to lose employees to other businesses that are offering the benefit? I suggest that this will change the playing field for many employers.

A strategic time for your business

How you respond is one of the most strategic decisions you can make for your business and requires some serious planning. I recommend educating yourself on the topic thoroughly before moving forward. The best idea is to meet with a professional that is very well versed on the topic and put together a detailed game plan before 2014 arrives.

Some businesses will be eligible to purchase their group insurance through the new exchange, which will be set up either by the state or federal government. Many employers who are accustomed to having an agent walk them through the process of selecting a plan and implementing it to their employees will now try to chart the waters without this assistance. There will also be many health insurance agents that will now go into the world of consulting to help employers navigate through the confusing world of health insurance starting in 2014. This will probably result in additional fees to employers.

As we have already seen at the time of publishing of this book, this law is constantly changing. We encourage you to continue to check back with us regularly as our team of Certified ObamaCare Advisors continuously stays up to date on all the changes and how they impact your business.

10
The Glass is Half Full: Three Benefits of ObamaCare

Often, we hear most about the negative impacts of this legislation, especially to business owners. There are some positives, however, that I would like to point out so it will help us all try to better cope with this new law of the land.

Tax incentives for small-/medium-sized businesses

As mentioned in Chapter 5, there are some tax incentives for some businesses to offer health insurance. These are currently in place today, allowing a business to write off some of the costs of their contributions towards employee health insurance and these incentives are set to increase in 2014. While the incentive is not enough to completely offset the offering of benefits, for some employers it is enough of an incentive to afford them to offer benefits, which allows them to attract and retain better employees.

Increased employee awareness and gratitude

With the changes requiring health insurance premiums paid by the employer to be shown on the W-2 form, this now gives employees another reminder of what is being paid on their behalf by employers. Many employees grow complacent with their benefits and do not realize the sacrifice that is being made by their employer to provide those benefits. This change now makes them aware just how much the annual cost is to provide those benefits. The Summary of Benefits that is now required to be distributed to employees is also a powerful tool. Of course, this is now a requirement for businesses to provide, which is some extra work; however, it does help to better inform employees of what coverage they have and how to use it best.

Employee stress reduction

One of the most stressful events in a person's life is trying to address the need for health insurance. This kind of stress and looming worry can in turn have a negative impact in the workplace. Maybe it isn't an employee who is directly dealing with not being able to secure health insurance, it may be his spouse or child, but it can absolutely be a driving force in his lack of productivity at work. By making it now a requirement for insurers to accept individuals, no matter what their pre-existing condition, this will no longer be a worry for employees. If you were already providing a group health insurance policy, this may not have applied to you; however, this will open more doors for those that were previously uninsurable to now obtain coverage.

Are You Ready? More Critical Questions

The following are some of our most commonly asked questions regarding ObamaCare readiness. Join me on my free 45-minute webinar to learn simple solutions to these questions and have the opportunity to ask some of your own. **Visit ObamaCareWebinar.com to secure your seat today.**

1. What does it matter if I am considered a large or small employer—this legislation will get me one way or the other, right?
2. How should I determine whether to decrease my full-time staff and increase my part-time staff?
3. What are some recommendations to help navigate the 90-day mandatory enrollment?
4. Can you explain the new regulations on the premium assistance tax credit?
5. Should I drop my current insurance carrier and go with an exchange?
6. How should I communicate changes to my employees?

About Chuck Kimball

Chuck Kimball is the Vice President of **Payday**, one of America's most progressive human resource outsourcing companies. Before joining Payday, Chuck began his professional career in such diverse industries as real estate, financial services, and training for a regional software company. His experience includes more than 15 years in human resources.

In 2006, Chuck earned his Professional in Human Resources (PHR) accreditation and is actively involved in both local and national chapters of the Society for Human Resource Management (SHRM). Additionally, Chuck's insurance background includes holding Health, Life, and Variable Annuity licenses as well as General Lines Property and Casualty licenses. He also holds many other safety designations and training certifications that contribute to his expertise in workforce management.

About the 24/7 Institute

The purpose of the **24/7 Institute** is to help you simplify your business.

Through high-content eBooks, books, webinars and seminars, we provide the simple business wisdom you need to successfully navigate the complexities of leading and growing your business.

Our consultants and speakers are among the best and most dynamic in business today. With a client list that is a Who's Who in industry (including Ford, IBM, Best Buy, Walmart, and dozens more), the 24/7 Institute can bring you the wisdom, insight and hands-on tools your team needs to blow past your competition!

So whether you are in healthcare, manufacturing, hospitality, or any other industry, our experts can bring the simple solutions you need to take your leadership, your business and your people to a higher level of success.

About Payday

The 24/7 Institute is sponsored by **Payday**, one of America's most progressive human resource outsourcing company. Payday's payroll, employee benefits, safety, workers' compensation and related services offer you the very best in managing and maximizing your company's most precious asset—your people. Learn more by visiting our website www.paydayhr.com.

Made in the USA
Monee, IL
04 November 2026

67382572R00026